Instant
Bible Lessons for
Preschoolers

I Am God's Child

by Pamela J. Kuhn

Rainbow Books

Rainbow Publishers • P.O. Box 261129 • San Diego, CA 92196

To Kent Stetler, who really loves being one of God's children every day.

INSTANT BIBLE LESSONS FOR PRESCHOOLERS: I AM GOD'S CHILD
©2001 by Rainbow Publishers, third printing
ISBN 1-885358-58-X

Rainbow Publishers
P.O. Box 261129
San Diego, CA 92196

Illustrator: Chuck Galey
Editor: Christy Allen
Cover Design: Stray Cat Studio, San Diego, CA

Scriptures are from the *Holy Bible: New International Version* (North American Edition), copyright ©1973, 1978, 1984 by the International Bible Society. Used by permission of Zondervan Bible Publishers.

Printed in the United States of America

Contents

Introduction

What is God's child like? Your preschoolers will be able to tell you that God's child is loving, kind, friendly, obedient, patient, thankful, content and happy after they have enjoyed the lessons in *I Am God's Child.* Your lively students will be eager to do all they can to please Jesus as they learn the truths in these lessons.

Each of the first eight chapters includes a Bible story, memory verse and numerous activities to help reinforce the truth in the lesson. An additional chapter contains miscellaneous projects that can be used anytime throughout the study or at the end to "recap" the lessons. Teacher aids are also sprinkled throughout the book, including bulletin board ideas and discussion starters.

The most exciting aspect of the *Instant Bible Lessons for Preschoolers* series, which includes *I Am God's Child, God's Servants Teach Me, I Belong to Jesus* and *I Learn Respect,* is its flexibility. You can easily adapt these lessons to a Sunday school hour, a children's church service, a Wednesday night Bible study or family home use. And because there is a variety of reproducible ideas from which to choose, you will enjoy creating a class session that is best for your group of students, whether larger or small, beginning or advanced, active or studious. Plus, the intriguing topics will keep your kids coming back for more, week after week.

This book is written to add fun and uniqueness to learning while reinforcing what it means to be God's child. Teaching children is exciting and rewarding, and in using I Am God's Child you, too, will find yourself becoming a better child of God.

How to Use This Book

Each chapter begins with a Bible story which you may read to your class, followed by discussion questions. Then, use any or all of the activities in the chapter to help drive home the message of that lesson. All of the activities are tagged with one of the icons below, so you can quickly flip through the chapter and select the projects you need. Simply cut off the teacher instructions on the pages and duplicate as desired.

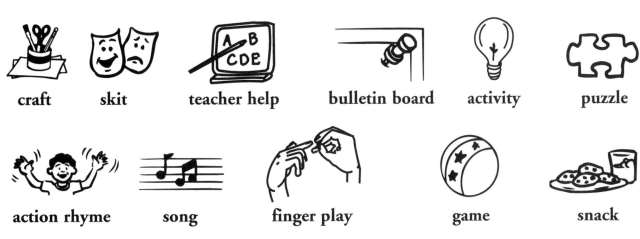

craft   skit   teacher help   bulletin board   activity   puzzle

action rhyme   song   finger play   game   snack

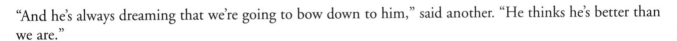

Chapter 1
God's Child Is Kind

Memory Verse

[Love] is not rude. 1 Corinthians 13:5

Story to Share
Speak Kindly, Joseph

Joseph's brothers hated him. "Father always treats Joseph better than he treats us," one of his older brothers said.

"Yes," agreed another. "Look at that coat he made for Joseph. Every color in the rainbow is in it."

"And he's always dreaming that we're going to bow down to him," said another. "He thinks he's better than we are."

One day, when no one else was around, the brothers took Joseph and sold him as a slave and he was taken to Egypt. He had to live in a new country with new people. But Joseph took someone with him — God was with Joseph even in this strange place.

God helped Joseph to see that a famine was coming. The king put Joseph in charge of saving food for the time of the famine. When food became scarce, Egypt still had food. Joseph was in charge of giving it to the needy.

Joseph's brothers became hungry. "Let's go to Egypt and get some food," they said. The brothers didn't know Joseph would be the one to give them the food.

Joseph could have refused to give them food or even ordered them to be killed. Instead, when he saw his brother he said, "God be good to you, my son."

Instead of angry words, Joseph used kind, courteous words. Joseph was God's child.

— based on Genesis 43:29

Questions for Discussion
1. What words are easy for you to say? Kind words? Angry words?
2. Which words please Jesus?

Kind Words

craft/song

• • • • • • • • • •

Materials
- puppet face pattern
- crayons
- scissors
- glue
- spring-type clothespins

Directions
1. Before class, duplicate and cut out a puppet face for each child.
2. Have the children color the face. Go around and cut apart each face on the dashed line.
3. Demonstrate how to glue the bottom of the face to the bottom of the clothespin. Then show how to glue the face top to the clothespin top.
4. Show how to squeeze the end of the clothespin to open and close while singing the song to the tune of "Row, Row, Row Your Boat."

God's Child Is Kind

God's Child
God's child is not rude,
Never, not one time.
So always use your manners and,
You'll get along just fine.

Joseph's Memory Verse

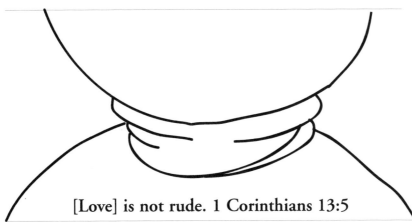

[Love] is not rude. 1 Corinthians 13:5

finished craft

Materials
- face and mouth patterns
- white paper lunch sacks
- glue
- crayons

Directions
1. Before class, duplicate and cut out a face and mouth for each student.
2. Have the children color the parts. They should also color the bag for the "coat of many colors."
3. Show the students how to glue the parts to the sack to make a puppet (see illustration).
4. Say, **Listen to what Joseph is saying, "Love is not rude." Can your Joseph say that to the friend sitting next to you?**

God's Child Is Kind

9

Rude or Kind?

puzzle

• • • • • • • • • • • •

Materials
• puzzle
• crayons

Directions
1. Before class, duplicate the puzzle for each child.
2. Use the discussion ideas below, then distribute the puzzles for the children to complete.

Discuss
Ask, **Do you know what it means to be rude? Here are some rude actions: pushing ahead in line; talking while someone else is talking; saying unkind words; taking the biggest cookie on the plate. What else can you think of?**

Which children below are being rude? God said, "Love is not rude." Draw a big X on the rude children. Draw and color a heart around the kind children.

God's Child Is Kind

10

Coat Window Decoration

craft

. . . .

Materials

- coat pattern
- liquid starch
- tissue paper, bright colors
- scissors
- glue
- yarn

Directions

1. Before class, duplicate and cut out two coats for each student. Cut yarn into 8" pieces.
2. Have the class help you tear tissue paper into strips.
3. Pour a teaspoon of starch in the middle of one of each child's coats.
4. Demonstrate how to spread the starch with your fingers over the front of the coat.
5. Show the students how to lay the strips in rows across the coat. Set aside to dry.
6. When the coats are dry, give each child a piece of yarn for a hanger and show how to place it on the back of the decorated coat then spread glue on the back of the other coat and glue the two together.

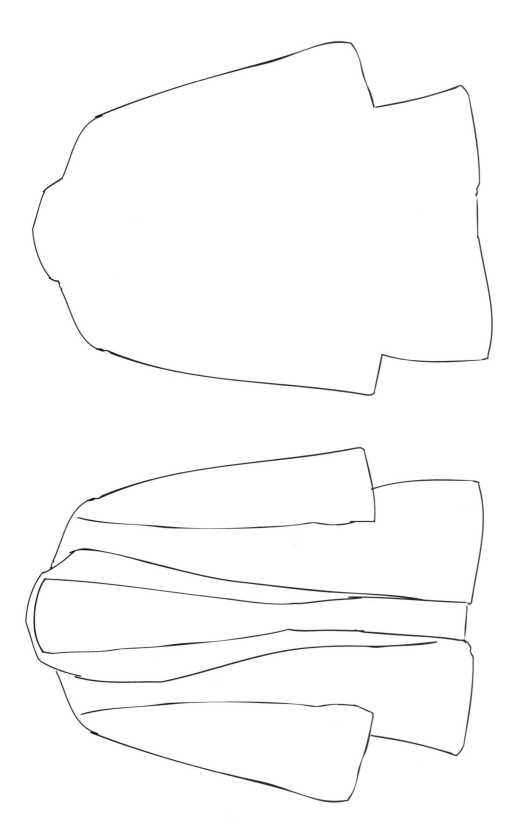

God's Child Is Kind

11

Snacks of Kindness

snack

• • • • • • • • • •

Materials
- saltine crackers
- peanut butter
- candy-coated buttons
- red shoestring licorice
- butterscotch chips
- waxed paper
- plastic knives

Directions

1. Give each child one waxed paper square, one cracker, one knife, one table-spoon of peanut butter, two candy-coated buttons, 3" of licorice and one butterscotch chip.
2. Demonstrate how to spread the peanut butter, then make smiling faces using the buttons for eyes, chip for nose and licorice for smile.
3. As the class enjoys the snack, discuss how kindness caus-es smiles.

Discuss
Ask, **What does the face of a rude person look like? Is it easy to smile when you are pushing someone or grab-bing the biggest treat? When you are kind you get a good feeling and your smile just can't stay away.**

God's Child Is Kind

Catch a Smile

game

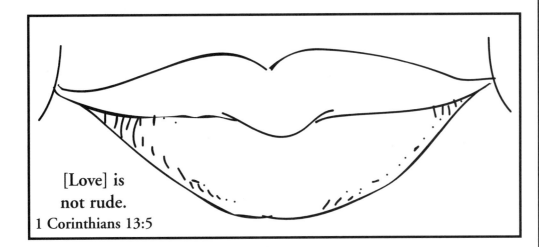

[Love] is
not rude.
1 Corinthians 13:5

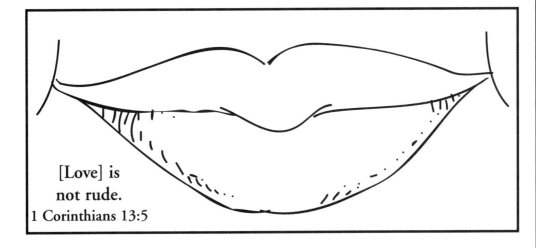

[Love] is
not rude.
1 Corinthians 13:5

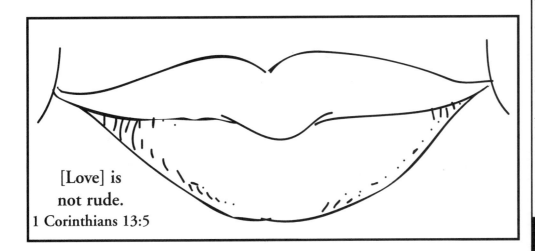

[Love] is
not rude.
1 Corinthians 13:5

Materials
- smile pattern
- red or pink crayons
- scissors
- string
- large magnet
- paper clips

Directions
1. Before class, duplicate and cut out the smiles and distribute them to the students to color.
2. Slip a paper clip onto each smile and lay them on the floor.
3. Tie 3" of string to the magnet. Allow each child to have a turn to "catch" a smile.

Discuss
Ask, **Do you know how to catch a smile? Be kind. When you hold the door for people, they say, "Thank you" and smile. When you say, "Excuse me" and move out of a friend's way, they say, "Thank you" and smile. But when you shove a friend, or grab toys out of another's hands, what happens? Instead of catching a smile, you catch a frown.**

God's Child Is Kind

13

activity

Materials
• activity sheet
• crayons

Directions

1. Before class, duplicate a frame for each student.
2. Have the students draw something with crayons that they did during the past week. They may also color the frames.
3. Allow time for the students to stand, hold up their picture and share what they drew.

Discuss

This lesson is that the children must be quiet and listen as the others describe their pictures. Say, **Being kind means you are quiet while others are talking. But you may nod your head while your friends are talking, and when they are through say, "That was very interesting."**

Usage

Make a picture of something you did during the week. Be the first to hold up the picture and talk about it. This will make it easier for the students to understand the activity.

God's Child Is Kind

Quiet Kindness

[Love] is not rude.
1 Corinthians 13:5

Verse Tracing

● ● ● ● ● ● ● ● ● ●

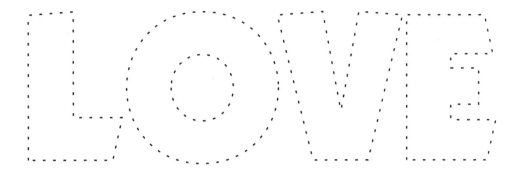

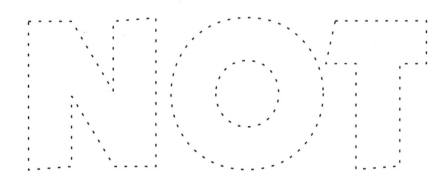

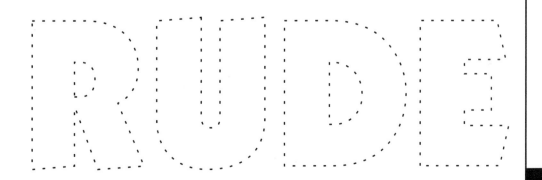

Materials
- activity sheet
- crayons

Directions
1. Before class, duplicate an activity sheet for each child.
2. Show how to trace the letters of the verse with a crayon. Say, **I will say the verse aloud while you are tracing, then you can say it with me.**
3. Ask, **Who was kind instead of rude in our Bible lesson today?**

God's Child Is Kind

Chapter 2
God's Child Is Friendly

Memory Verse

A friend loves at all times. Proverbs 17:17

Story to Share
Hi, Friend!

Jesus was taking a trip. He was going from Samaria to Judea. Jesus' disciples were with Him. "I'm getting hungry," one of them said.

"Let's rest here," said Jesus, pointing to a well. "We can get some food and drink."

Jesus' disciples went into the town to get some food. Jesus sat down on the edge of the well to rest and wait. A Samaritan woman came to the well to get some water.

"Hi!" said Jesus. "I'm thirsty. Could you give me a drink of water?"

The woman was surprised that Jesus talked to her. "Why are you talking to me? You are a Jew and Jews don't talk to Samaritans."

Jesus knew everyone was important to God, no matter who they were, what they looked like or what they owned. Not only did He drink the water she gave to Him, Jesus also told her how to be saved.

This woman was so excited she hurried to town. "Come and see!" she said. "Jesus is here."

Because Jesus was friendly to one woman, many others came and learned how to be saved. Jesus is God's child.

—based on John 4:1-39

Questions for Discussion
1. Do you like it when others are friendly to you?
2. When can you be friendly to others?

"How Do You Do" Chant

Usage

Say, **Listen to me as I chant this verse** (chant one time). **Now, why don't you try and say it with me?**

Discuss

Say, **Being friendly is simple.** Ask, **"How are you?"** and say, **"Jesus loves you!"**

Hi! How do you do?
Are you feeling sunny or blue?
Gu-ess What!
Jesus loves you,
And I do, too!
This is very
True,   True,   True!

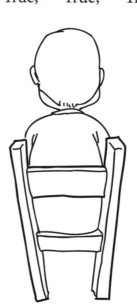

Hello at the Well

craft

. . . .

Materials

- Jesus, arm and well (p. 20) patterns
- scissors
- glue
- paper fasteners
- crayons

Directions

1. Before class, duplicate and cut out the pieces for each child.
2. Instruct the students to color the pieces.
3. Show where to glue Jesus to the well.
4. Go around and push the paper fastener through the holes. Allow the children to open the spikes.
5. Say, **Look, you can see how friendly Jesus is by waving His arm. Can you wave your arm and let someone know you are friendly?**

Discuss

Ask, **Do you think Jesus was friendly to everyone or only a few?** He didn't pick out the ones who had lots of money, or those who were beautiful. He was friendly to everyone. What about you?

God's Child Is Friendly

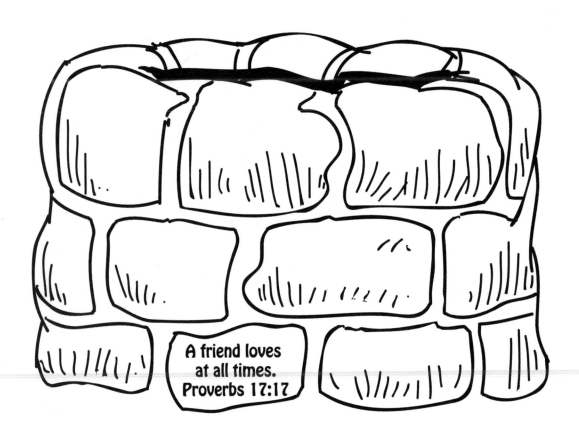

A friend loves
at all times.
Proverbs 17:17

Friendly Children

A friend loves
at all times.
Proverbs 17:17

Materials
- puzzle
- crayons
- scissors
- envelope

Directions
1. Before class, duplicate and cut out a puzzle for each child.
2. Instruct the children to color their puzzles, using as many colors as possible.
3. Cut the puzzle pieces apart for each student. Place the pieces in envelopes for the children to take home.

Discuss
Ask, **Who do you think is friendly? Are only the children from the United States friendly? What about Russian children? Latin American children? All God's children are friendly. You will be friendly if you are God's child.**

God's Child Is Friendly

activity

Materials
- telephone pattern
- scissors
- curling ribbon
- Velcro™

Directions

1. Before class, duplicate and cut out a phone for each child. Attach a small piece of Velcro™ to the Xs (this is where the receiver will attach to the base). Cut a 2" piece of ribbon for each child. Curl it with the edge of a scissors blade.
2. Show how to tape the ribbons to the black dots.
3. Gather the students in a circle. Choose a starting child. The student will pick up the receiver, dial the telephone and say, "Ring, Ring." The child to his left will pick up his receiver and says, "Hello." The first child will say, "A friend loves at all times." Then he hangs up his receiver. The second child will then ring the third and so on until each student has a turn.

Speaking to Your Friend

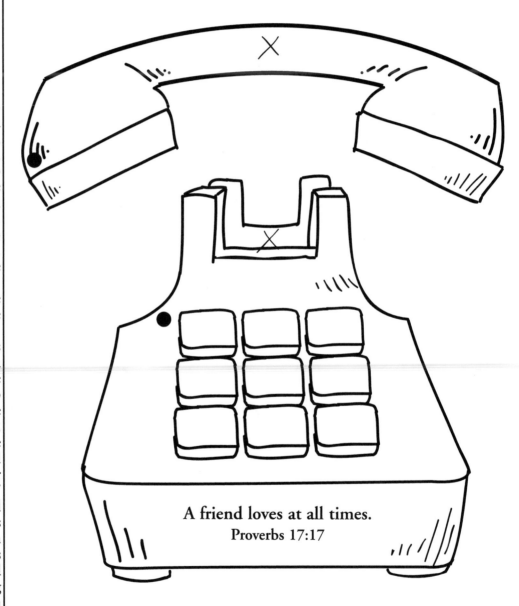

A friend loves at all times.
Proverbs 17:17

Friendship Tea Craft

craft

. . . .

Materials
- tag pattern
- lightweight inter-facing
- glue
- potpourri
- string
- clear tape

Directions
1. Before class, cut two 3" squares of inter-facing and duplicate the tag pattern for each child. Cut the string into 6" pieces.
2. Give each student two interfacing squares and one tablespoon of pot-pourri.
3. Demonstrate how to glue around all four edges of one square, putting the potpour-ri in the middle and pressing the other square on top of the first.
4. Go around the room and make sure all edges are pressed together to seal the squares.
5. Staple a piece of string to each child's tag and the other end to the bag. Cover the staples with tape to avoid injury.
(Use this with the Friendship Tea on page 24.)

God's Child Is Friendly

Friendship Tea

A friend loves at all times.
Proverbs 17:17

Friendship Tea

A friend loves at all times.
Proverbs 17:17

Friendship Tea

snack

· · · · · · · · · ·

Materials

- invitation
- crayons
- scissors
- soft bread
- cheese slices
- small cookie cutters
- tiny white cookies
- tube of frosting with star tip
- two cups of tea
- two cups of apple juice
- two cups of cranapple juice
- one cinnamon stick

Directions

1. Fill in the invitation before duplicating. Cut them out and have the children color them.
2. Use the cookie cutters to cut out the bread and cheese and make tiny sandwiches.
3. Combine the tea, juices and cinnamon stick in a crock pot. Simmer the drink until the party is ready.
4. Make an icing flower on each cookie.

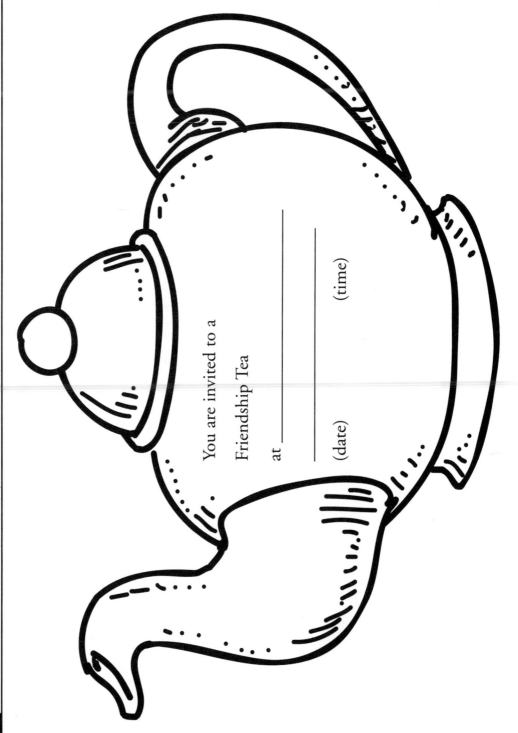

You are invited to a Friendship Tea

at _____ (date)

_____ (time)

A Man's Friend

A man speaks well with his friends.

Hello, how are you?
I'm glad you're my friend.

A man speaks well with his friends.
Will you be my friend every day? — Yeah! Yeah!

Directions

1. Sing the song to the tune of "Away Far Over Jordan."
2. On the second line, have the kids turn and shake hands with a neighbor.
3. On the last line ("Yeah! Yeah!") show how to punch a fist in the air.

Usage

Say, **Having friends makes us feel so good that we feel like shouting, "Yeah!" Try shouting, "Yeah!"**

God's Child Is Friendly

25

Chapter 3
God's Child Is Loving

Memory Verse

Love each other. 1 Thessalonians 4:9

Story to Share
Loving God's Prophet

Elijah was God's prophet. He knew that he would go to heaven one day and would need someone to take his place. "God," he prayed. "Who shall I choose to take my place?"

"Go find Elisha," God told him. "He will take your place as prophet."

Elijah found Elisha in the field. He had twelve yoke of oxen pulling his plow. When Elijah got close to Elisha, he took his own cloak and threw it over Elisha's shoulders.

Elisha bowed his head. He loved Elijah and was honored to take his place. "I don't feel worthy," he whispered. With the prophet's cloak around his shoulders, he left his plow and followed Elijah to become a prophet.

One day after Elijah had gone to heaven, Elisha went to Shunem. While he was there he met a rich man and woman. "Come, eat with us," they invited.

Elisha went to their home. "Thank you," he said after eating the delicious fruits and other good food. "The meal was so good."

"Come anytime," the couple urged. "We have an extra room just for you."

They gave Elisha his own room on the cool roof. The room had a bed, a stool, a table and a lamp. It was a special place for Elisha to rest.

"This Shunemite couple is so loving," said Elisha. "I wish I knew what I could do to show my love for them."

"I know," a friend told Elisha. "This lady would like to have a son."

Elisha told the woman, "You shall have a son."

What a joy the son was to the Shunemite woman. She and her husband loved a prophet of God. In return, Elisha was loving to them. They were God's children.

— based on 2 Kings 4:8-17

Questions for Discussion
1. Do you think being loving encourages others to show love to you?
2. The Shunemite couple showed love to Elisha. Was he loving in return?
3. How can you show love to those who have shown love to you?

What's Wrong with Elisha's Room?

What's wrong with Elisha's room? There should be five things that would have been strange to find in Elisha's room. Circle the strange sights, then color the picture.

Materials
• activity sheet
• crayons

Directions

1. Before class, duplicate the puzzle for each child.
2. After the children have finished the puzzle discuss each thing that is wrong in the picture.

Discuss

Ask, **Did the Shunemite couple have strange things in Elisha's room? No, they wanted everything to be perfect for the one they loved. They did their best.**

Answers

1. basketball hoop
2. plant in bed
3. in-line skates
4. lamp
5. Elisha's handstand

God's Child Is Loving

Three in a Row

game

Materials
- cards
- crayons
- glue
- scissors
- colored marshmallows
- poster board

Directions
1. Before class, duplicate and cut out a set of cards for each student. Cut out one set of cards for yourself.
2. Instruct the children to color the squares, then glue them on the poster board in any pattern. Do not glue yours.
3. Turn your cards upside-down. As you show each square, assist the students in covering the correct one on their game boards with a marshmallow. Ask the students to identify the meaning of the picture to the story.
4. The first one with three in a row wins.

Usage
Have extra marshmallows on hand because many will be eaten during the game!

Loving Goes Both Ways

craft

· · · · · · · · · · · ·

Materials
- card and heart patterns
- red construction paper
- scissors
- crayons
- glue
- flannel, two patterns

Directions

1. Before class, duplicate and cut out a heart from red construction paper and the cards for each student. Cut each kind of flannel into small pieces.
2. Instruct the students to color the pictures.
3. Show where to glue the flannel on the cards for the baby's blanket and a cover for the bed.
4. Show how to glue the backs of the cards to the front and back of the heart.
5. Show how to work the book. Ask, **How did the Shunemite couple show love to Elisha? How did Elisha show his love to the Shunemite couple?**

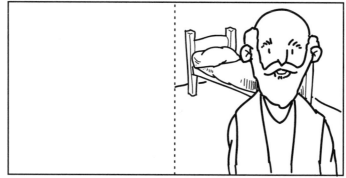

finished craft

Food for Elisha

Love each other.

1 Thessalonians 4:9

Materials
- box pattern
- crayons
- clear tape
- scissors
- dates, nuts, grapes and cheese cubes

Directions
1. Before class, duplicate and cut out one box per child. Slice the dashed lines in the corners.
2. Allow the children to color the box.
3. Demonstrate how to fold the box on the dashed lines and tape the flaps together.
4. Fill the boxes with dates, nuts, grapes and cheese cubes for the snack.

God's Child Is Loving

Love Each Other

. . . .

Directions

1. Sing the song to the tune of "Ten Little Indians."
2. Hold up fingers as you count.
3. At the end of each time you sing the chorus, pick a child to share a way he or she can show love to someone.

Discuss

Ask, **Do you have anyone who loves you? How do they show their love? Does God love you? How does He show His love? How can you be loving this week?**

One little, two little, three little
ways to love.
Four little, five little, six little
ways to love.
Seven little, eight little, nine little
ways to love.
Ten ways to love each other.

God's Child Is Loving

32

Loving Chores

♡ CHORE CHART ♡

MONDAY

TUESDAY

WEDNESDAY

THURSDAY

FRIDAY

SATURDAY

SUNDAY

Love each other.
1 Thessalonians 4:9

Materials
- chore chart and cards
- glue
- crayons

Directions
1. Before class, duplicate and cut out the chore chart and cards, one set per child.
2. Hand out the chore charts and cards and instruct the students to color them.
3. Demonstrate how to fold the charts on the dashed line and glue the edges to form a pocket to hold the cards.

Discuss
Say, **One of the places you can show love is at home. When you do your chores cheerfully, it makes the day go better for your mother and father. This week, do a loving chore each day. When your chore is finished, glue or tape the card to your chart.**

God's Child Is Loving

Loving Gift

craft

Materials
- flower and tag
- crayons
- pencils, unsharpened
- curling ribbon, green
- scissors
- yellow pompons
- glue
- hole punch

Directions
1. Before class, duplicate and cut out a flower and a tag per student. Cut a 20" piece of ribbon and curl the ends for each child.
2. Give each child a flower to color.
3. Show how to curve the petals by rolling them on a pencil.
4. Instruct the students to glue a pompon to the center of the flower.
5. Go around and punch holes in the tag and tie it to each flower.

Discuss
Say, **When we give gifts to people we make them feel loved. The Shunemite couple made Elisha feel loved when they gave him the special room. Elisha made them feel loved when he gave them the baby. We can make someone feel loved by giving them this gift.**

God's Child Is Loving

YOU
ARE
LOVED

Loving Partners

activity

Materials
- hearts
- scissors

Directions
1. Before class, duplicate and cut the hearts apart on the lines.
2. As each child arrives, give him or her half a heart.
3. Instruct the students to find the child who has the other piece to the heart they have. They will be partners for the class.

Chapter 4
God's Child Is Obedient

Memory Verse

We will obey. Joshua 24:24

Story to Share
Joshua Obeys God

"God, show me what to do," prayed Joshua. "I am nearing Jericho. How can we conquer the city with those high, high walls?"

God told Joshua what to do. But what a strange command God gave him! Would it really work? Joshua didn't hesitate, he went right to the captains of his army. "God has told me how to conquer Jericho," he said.

When the captains heard what God said, they agreed: "It is very strange, but we will do what God has commanded."

The next day all of the soldiers of Joshua's army lined up. Joshua led the army in a line around the city of Jericho as God commanded. They marched all around the city and they did not say a word. There were hundreds and hundreds of soldiers and they were all quiet.

For six days the soldiers marched around the city and for six days they were quiet. On the seventh day, Joshua's army marched around the city seven times. Seven times around and not one sound was heard! But then, the trumpets blew and the soldiers yelled as loud as they could.

As all the noise hit the air, the walls of Jericho came tumbling down. The soldiers rushed into the city and destroyed it.

The walls fell down because Joshua obeyed God. He was God's child.

— based on Joshua 5:13-6:26

Questions for Discussion
1. Is it always easy to obey?
2. Should we always obey?
3. Who in our Bible Story obeyed God?

action rhyme

• • • • • • • • • • •

Usage
Direct the class to form a circle. Demonstrate the rhyme first, repeating it several times.

Obedient Joshua

Around and around the army went.   *march in place*

Shh, Shh, don't say a word.   *finger to lips*

One, two, three, four, five, six days.   *count on fingers*

Around and around not a sound was heard.   *march in place*

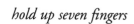

On day seven the army marched around.   *march in place*

Shh, Shh, don't say a word.   *finger to lips*

Seven times, shh, shh, don't say a word.   *hold up seven fingers*

Around and around not a sound was heard.   *march in place*

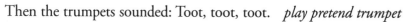

Then the trumpets sounded: Toot, toot, toot.   *play pretend trumpet*

The army men shouted: Yeah, yeah, yeah.   *hands to mouth*

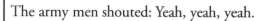

The walls fell down: Crash, crash, crash.   *clap hands*

What a happy, happy day.   *big smiles*

God's Child Is Obedient

38

Edible Walls

We Will Obey

Joshua 24:24

We Will Obey

Materials
- flag pattern
- toothpicks
- glue
- graham crackers
- canned icing, peanut butter flavor
- waxed paper
- plastic knives
- large marshmallows

Directions
1. Before class, duplicate and cut out one flag for each student.
2. Show the students how to fold a flag in half and glue it around a toothpick.
3. Have them stick the flag in a marshmallow.
4. Demonstrate how to form walls and a roof with the graham crackers squares and icing.
5. Show how to spread a small amount of icing on the bottom of the marshmallow and stick it to center of the "roof."

God's Child Is Obedient

activity

Materials
- activity sheet
- scissors
- crayons
- glue

Directions

1. Before class, duplicate the soldiers on the activity sheet and cut out one set per child. Then duplicate the walled Jericho picture for each child.
2. Give each child a worksheet and discuss obedience (see below).
3. Instruct the class to choose the soldiers who are being obedient and glue them in place on the picture.
4. Allow them to color the picture.

Discuss

Say, **When you obey your parents, you do exactly what they tell you to do. When Joshua's soldiers obeyed God, they did exactly what God told Joshua they should do. How can we obey God better?**

God's Child Is Obedient

God's Soldiers

We will obey.

Joshua 24:24

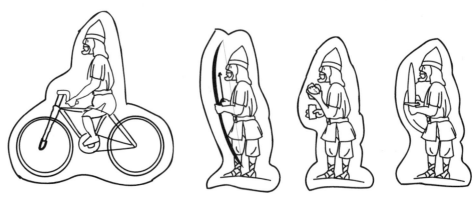

Obedience Puzzle

puzzle

Materials

- puzzle pattern
- poster board
- scissors
- crayons

Directions

1. Before class, duplicate the puzzle pieces on poster board or glue them to poster board and cut them out, one set per child.
2. Instruct the students to solve the puzzle and color it.

Usage

This is a good project for free time at the beginning of your class session. Place a couple of sets of puzzles around the table for those who arrive early.

We Will Obey

Materials
- Bible page pattern
- black construction paper
- crayons
- glitter pen, gold
- glue

Directions

1. Duplicate and cut out the page for each child. Fold in half (book-style) a sheet of black construction paper for each one.
2. Give each child a copy of the Bible page and instruct them to trace the verse. Say it together as you trace.
3. Show how to glue the Bible page to the inside of the folded black construction paper.
4. Show the students how to draw a cross on the cover with the glitter pen. Allow the Bibles to dry.

Discuss

Say, **Do you know what Book this is? The Bible! God gives us rules to obey. Can you think of any rules in the Bible?**

God's Child Is Obedient

WE WILL OBEY

Joshua 24:24

Obedience Trophy

_____ was obedient today.

Date _____

Teacher _____

We will obey. Joshua 24:24

craft

Materials
- soldier pattern
- scissors
- crayons

Directions
1. Before class, duplicate and cut out one soldier per child.
2. Give the students a soldier and instruct them to color it.
3. Demonstrate how to fold back the dashed-line tabs on the soldier so it will stand.

God's Child Is Obedient

Stand-Up Soldier

Will You Obey?

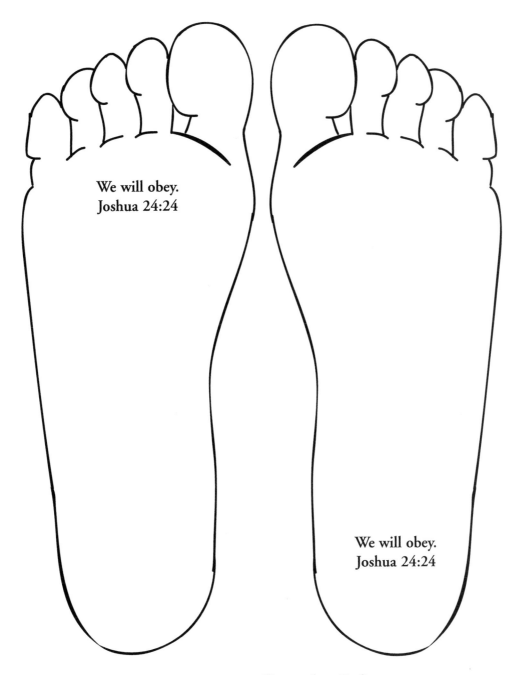

We will obey.
Joshua 24:24

We will obey.
Joshua 24:24

Emmy, Emmy, will you obey God?
Emmy, Emmy, will you obey God?
Emmy, Emmy, will you obey God?
Oh, will your feet obey?

Emmy says, "I will obey God!"
Emmy says, "I will obey God!"
Emmy says, "I will obey God!"
"Yes my feet will obey."

Materials

- feet patterns
- scissors

Directions

1. Duplicate and cut out one set of feet and place them on the floor. Also make a set for each child.
2. Choose a child to stand on the feet.
3. Sing the song to the tune of "Skip To My Lou" using each child's name in place of Lou.
4. Give each child a set of obedience feet to take home.

Discuss

Ask, **Do you ever have trouble obeying? Do your feet ever want to say, "No?" Take these feet home and put them in a corner of your room. When your feet want to say, "No," go stand on your obedience feet and remember this song.**

God's Child Is Obedient

Chapter 5
God's Child Is Patient

Memory Verse

Be patient. James 5:7

Story to Share

Abraham Has Patience

Abraham lived in a city called Ur. One day God spoke to him. "Abraham, I want you to move. I will show you where I want you to live."

Abraham chose to do just what God told him to do. God was pleased and made a promise to him. "I will make your people a great people, Abraham. I will bless you and make your name great. Everyone here on earth will be blessed because of you."

What a promise! Abraham and his family left Ur and traveled toward the place God chose for them to live. On the way, they stopped at a place called Moreh. Again God spoke to Abraham: "Abraham, I will give all this land to your children." In honor of God's promise, Abraham made an altar and worshipped God.

Abraham wondered how this land could belong to his children when he did not have any children. He was old and his wife, Sarah, was old.

Abraham and his family finally came to Canaan, the land where God wanted them to live. Again God spoke to Abraham: "Look up, Abraham. See all the stars in the sky?"

Abraham looked at the twinkling stars in sky. "Yes, Lord, there are many, many stars."

"You will have many in your family," promised God. "You will have children, your children will have children, and those children will have children. You will have more descendants than the stars in the sky. This land, Canaan, will belong to them."

Another big promise! But Abraham knew God always kept the promises He made. When Abraham was 100 years old, Sarah gave birth to a son.

It was hard for Abraham to wait 100 years for a son, but he had patience. He was God's child.

— based on Genesis 12:2; 17:1

Questions for Discussion

1. Do you like it when your mom or dad says, "Just a minute?"
2. Do you think you should learn to be patient now so when God wants you to wait you will find it easy to be patient?

God's Patient Stars

bulletin board

• • • • • • • • • •

Materials
- small and large star patterns
- paper: yellow, gold, dark blue and white
- gold paper
- scissors
- felt-tip marker
- fiberfill
- glitter pen
- cotton balls

Directions
1. Cover the bulletin board with dark blue paper.
2. Duplicate and cut out one large star for each child and for yourself from yellow paper.
3. Allow each student to trace along the edges of a star with the glitter pen.
4. Write each student's name on a star.
5. Post the stars on the bulletin board.
6. Attach fiberfill to the bottom of the board.
7. Duplicate and cut out the smaller stars from gold paper.
8. Stretch the cotton balls. Alternate the cotton and small stars around the sides of the board for a border.
9. Freehand cut or trace the letters "God's Stars" and attach them to the board as shown.

God's Child Is Patient

finished bulletin board

Patience Badge

craft

Dear Mom or Dad:
I'm learning how to be patient.
Abraham was patient when God promised him a large family.
I want to be patient, too. When you catch me being patient,
would you please clip the patient badge on me? Thank you.

XOXO,

_____

PATIENCE

Materials
- star patterns
- note to parents
- small star
- yellow paper
- poster board
- aluminum foil
- clothespins
- scissors
- glue

Directions
1. Duplicate and cut out the large star. Trace and cut one from poster board for each child. Duplicate the small star on yellow paper and cut out one per student. Duplicate the note to parents for each child.
2. Give each student a poster board star and a piece of foil slightly larger than the star.
3. Show how to fold the foil around the star.
4. Show where to glue the yellow star on the foil star.
5. Instruct them to glue a clothespin to the back and allow it to dry.
6. Say, **Your parents will allow you to wear your badge when you are patient.**
7. Pass out the notes and help the children write their names on them.

puzzle

Materials
- activity sheet
- yellow crayons
- flannel

Directions
1. Before class, dupli- cate the activity sheet for each child. Cut a small piece of flannel for each student.
2. Have the children color the stars with a yellow crayon, then glue the flannel on Isaac's blanket.

Usage
Have this activity ready for those extra minutes while you are preparing for another activity. There are 56 stars in the picture.

Hidden Stars

How many stars can you find in the picture?

Folding Starry Sky

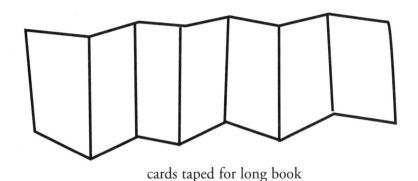

cards taped for long book

craft

- - - - - - - - - -

Materials
- book cover pattern
- 4" x 6" plain index cards
- clear tape
- scissors
- glue
- star stickers
- star stamp and stamp pad

Directions
1. Prepare a book for each child before class by folding three index cards in half. Open the cards and tape them together at the sides to form a long book (see at left). Write "God's Promise to Abraham" along the bottoms of the books. Duplicate and cut out a book cover for each child.
2. Show the children how to glue the book cover to the front.
3. Say, **God makes promises to you, but you must be patient and wait. He promises you a beautiful home in heaven. What are some other promises of God?**
4. Show the children how to fill their book sky with stars: either stickers or stamps.
5. Count with the students to see how many stars they have in the skies of their books.

BE PATIENT

BE PATIENT

God's Child Is Patient

Be Patient

Directions

1. Form a circle and hold hands.
2. Stand in the center of the circle and sing the song to the tune of "Old McDonald's Farm."
3. Drop hands at the phrase "star here" and twinkle your hands above your head.
4. When the song is over, point to a child to join you in the circle. Continue until all of the children are in the circle.

God wants us to be patient,
Yes, O, Yes, He does.
God wants us to be patient,
Yes, O, Yes, He does.

With a star here,
And a star there,
Here a star,
There a star,
Everywhere a star, star,
God wants us to be patient,
Yes, O, Yes, He does.

God's Child Is Patient

Star Dust Juice

snack

· · · · · · · · · · ·

Materials

- cup decoration pattern
- scissors
- crayons
- foam cups
- glue
- three cups of pineapple juice
- two bananas
- one cup of lemon-lime soda
- blender

Directions

1. Before class, duplicate and cut out a cup decoration for each child.
2. Instruct the children to color all of the stars on the decoration.
3. Show the students how to spread glue on the rim of the cup and press the decoration in place.
4. Measure juice, bananas and soda into a blender.
5. Give each student a turn at pushing the blend button.
6. Write the students' names on the bottoms of the cups to avoid mix-ups. Pour juice into cups. The recipe serves about eight small children.

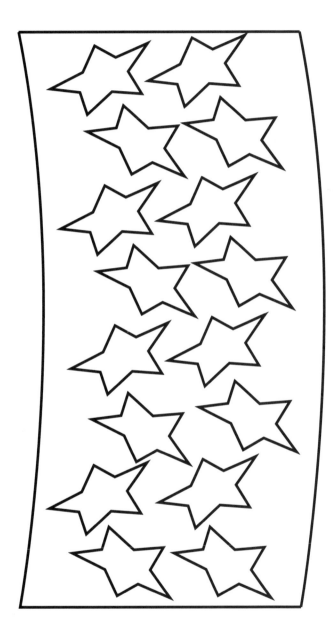

Prayer

Thank you, God, for the stars,
Twinkling above me.

And for this special star dust juice,
I bow my head and thank thee. Amen

God's Child Is Patient

53

Finish the Picture

Materials
- activity sheet
- crayons

Directions
1. Before class, duplicate the page for each child.
2. Give each child a picture. Explain the following instructions:
a. Draw a tent by Abraham.
b. Draw five stars in the sky.
c. Draw a moon in the sky.
d. Fill in Abraham's face.
e. Color the picture.

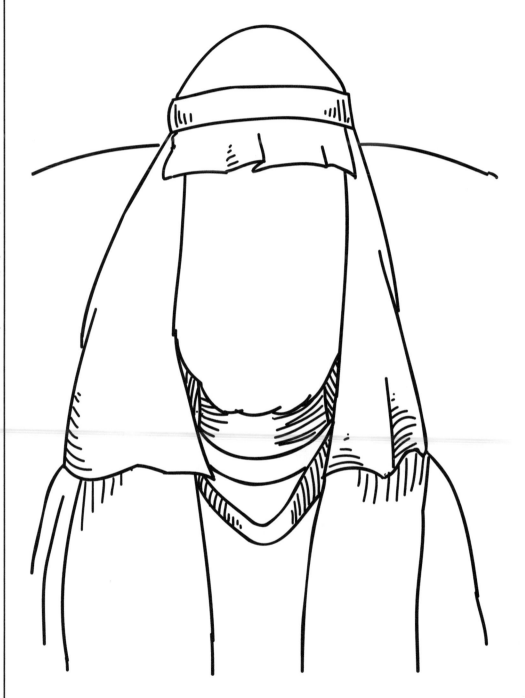

Be patient.
James 5:7

More Than All of These

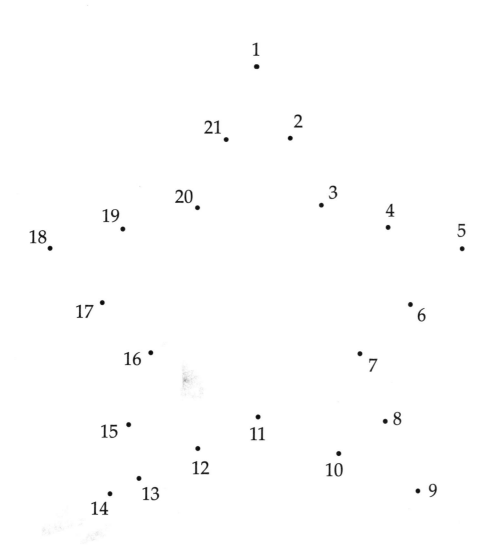

1

21   2

20   3   4   5

19

18

17   6

16   7

15   11   8

12   10

13   9

14

Be patient.
James 5:7

Materials
- puzzle
- crayons

Directions
1. Before class, duplicate the puzzle for each child.
2. Say, **God told Abraham he would have more family than all the _____. Connect the dots to find out the answer. Then color the surprise.**

Chapter 6
God's Child Is Thankful

Memory Verse

Give thanks. 1 Thessalonians 5:18

Story to Share
Thank You, Jesus

"Did you hear?" asked one man.

"Hear what?" another answered.

"That Jesus is coming through here," said the first.

At the words of the man, nine other men were suddenly as still as mice. Finally one spoke, "Jesus is coming, you say?"

These ten men had leprosy, a terrible sickness, and they had heard wonderful things about Jesus and His power to heal. Could it be possible they would be healed? The lepers were filled with hope as they quickly walked as close to the road as they were allowed.

Lepers were not allowed to be near the road where people would be walking because they were afraid of catching the dreaded disease. So when the lepers saw Jesus, they had to call loudly, "Jesus, Jesus, please have mercy on us. Take away our leprosy, Jesus."

Jesus turned and looked at the men. Their capes had hoods that covered their heads. They had scarves around their faces. This was so no one would have to look at their horrible sores.

"Yes," answered Jesus. "I will heal you. Go and show the priests that you are healed of your disease."

The ten men ran quickly toward town. They knew that as soon as the priest saw that they were healed from their dreadful disease they could go back home.

All of a sudden, one man stopped. Jesus had healed him and he had forgotten to even say thank You. Running back to where Jesus was, he kneeled down. "Jesus, thank You, thank You for healing me," he said.

Jesus looked around. "It is good that you are thankful, but where are the others? Didn't I heal ten lepers?"

Only one healed leper was thankful. He was God's child.

— based on Luke 17:12-19

Questions for Discussion

1. Do you sometimes forget to thank God for what He does for you?
2. What can you thank God for?

activity

Materials
- spots
- safety scissors
- two-sided tape

Directions
1. Duplicate a sheet of spots for each child.
2. Have the students cut out the spots.
3. Show how to put a small piece of tape to the spot and then stick it to an arm.
4 Say, **I'm going to tell this story; can you brush your spots off when the lepers are healed?**

Healed Leprosy

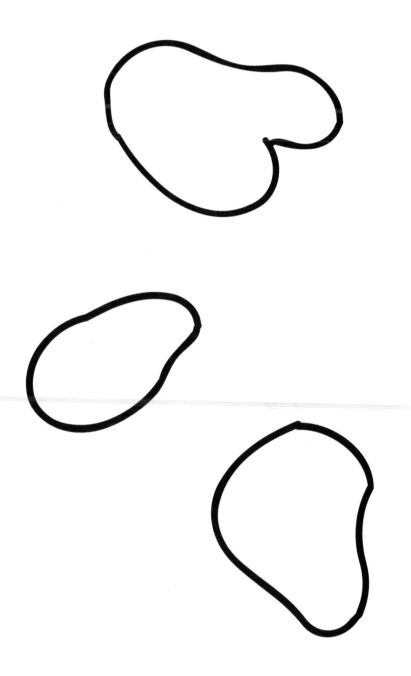

Thankful Leper Runs Back

craft/song

. . . .
Materials

- leper pattern
- scissors
- crayons

Directions

1. Before class, duplicate and cut out a leper finger puppet for each child. Cut out the leg openings.
2. Instruct the students to color the lepers.
3. Demonstrate how to put your fingers through the holes of the puppet and make the leper run.
4. Sing the song to the tune of "Row, Row, Row Your Boat," allowing the leper to run toward town, then run him back to say "Thank You," kneeling in front of Jesus.

Song

Run, run, run to town.
Tell the happy news.
Oops, I forgot to thank my Lord.
I stop and turn around.

Run, run, run to say,
Thank You, precious Lord.
Thank You for Your healing touch.
Praise your name today!

puzzle

Materials

- maze
- poster board
- clear, self-stick plastic
- grease pencil
- string
- hole punch
- soft cloth

Directions

1. Duplicate and cover the maze with the self-stick plastic.
2. Punch a hole on the X. Tie string to the maze and to a grease pencil.
3. Lay the maze on the table for early arrivals to enjoy. Place a soft cloth beside it so it can be used over and over.

Usage

For a large class you may wish to make two or three copies of the maze. This maze may also be duplicated for a class worksheet.

Going Back

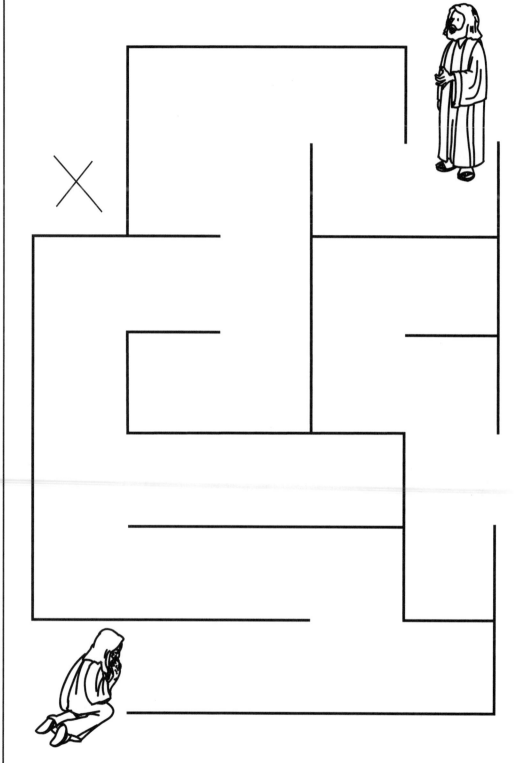

Give Thanks

game

• • • • • • • • • •

Materials
- circles
- colored paper
- poster board
- scissors

Directions

1. Duplicate the circle twice on colored paper. Trace them on poster board and cut out the poster board circles. Glue the poster board to the backs of the paper circles. Write "Give" in the center of one and "Thanks" in the center of the other.

2. Lay the circles on the floor, one foot apart.

3. Demonstrate how to jump on "Give" and say, "Give," then jump to "Thanks" and say, "Thanks."

4. Allow each student a chance to jump and say the verse, then move the circles another 6" apart. Continue moving the circles apart as far as the students can jump.

5. The circles may be duplicated for each child to have a game to take home.

God's Child Is Thankful

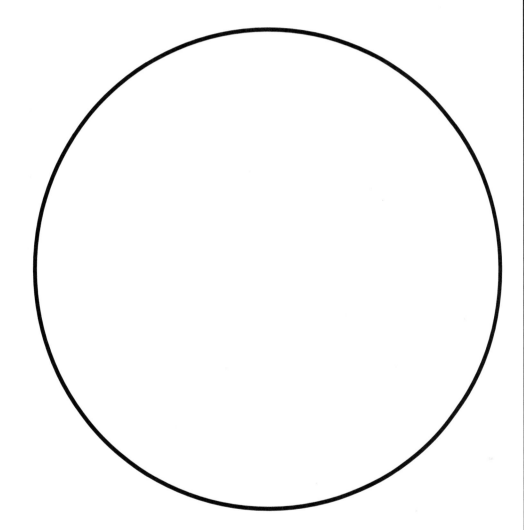

61

craft

Materials
- streamer patterns
- yarn
- scissors
- glue
- crayons
- crepe paper streamers
- hole punch

Directions
1. Before class, duplicate the streamer patterns and cut out a set for each child. Cut the crepe paper into one 18" length for each child.
2. Instruct the students to color the streamer pieces.
3. Give each child a crepe paper streamer. Show how to glue the praying hands at the top of the streamer and the things they are thankful for below the hands.
4. Go around the room and punch a hole where indicated on the praying hands.
5. Have the students help you tie a yarn hanger through the hole.

Usage
This is a good project to do after completing the lesson, "I'm Thankful For…"

Thankfulness Streamer

I'M THANKFUL FOR

Class Mural

• • • • • • • • • •

Materials
- bow and hat patterns
- poster paper
- crayons: black and assorted

Directions
1. Cover one wall with poster paper. Say, **What would you do if you were the only student in our class? It would be lonely, wouldn't it? You should be thankful for the friends in this room.**
2. Stand a child with his or her back to the poster paper. Trace around the child with black crayon.
3. Instruct the child to color in the clothes and fill in the face and hair to make the shape look like him or her.
4. Continue with each child.
5. Give each girl a bow and boy a hat. Instruct the girls to glue the bow in their "twin's" hair and the boys to glue the hat on their "twin's" head.
6. Write above the children, "Thank you for our friends."

God's Child Is Thankful

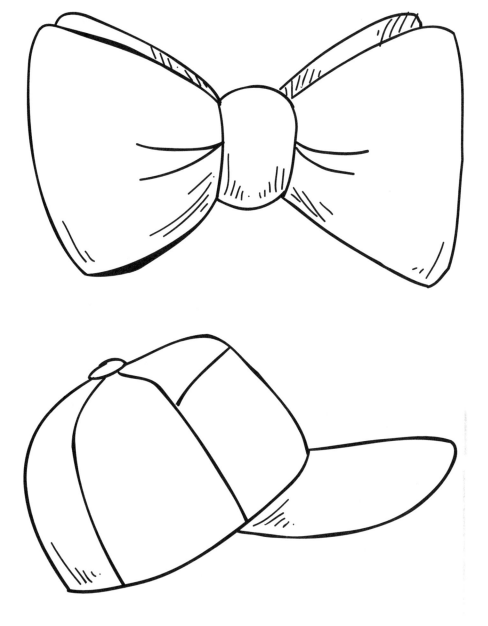

activity

Materials

- thankful items
- graham cracker strips
- raisins
- dried apples

Directions

1. Duplicate and cut out the thankful items.
2. Lay all of them, except the food, face down on the table.
3. One-by-one have a child pick up a paper, and say, "I am thankful for…"
4. When the last item is chosen, hold up the food and say, **I am thankful for food, are you? I have a snack for all of you, so let's thank God for all these things, and let's thank Him for our snack, too.**

Usage

Say, **Jesus, we want to thank You for all of the blessings You give us. We thank You for** _____ (allow the child who picked the item to fill in the word).

I'm Thankful For...

Lots of Thanks

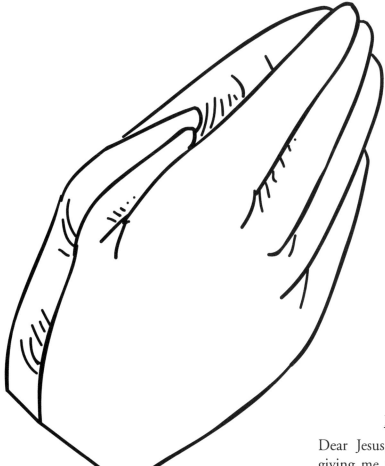

. . . .

Materials
- large and small praying hands patterns
- large coffee can
- cotton balls
- crayons
- resealable plastic bags
- scissors
- glue
- large foam cups

Directions
1. Before class, cut out the large praying hands, color and glue to the side of the can. Duplicate the small praying hands for each child. Count out 10 cotton balls per student (one for each leper) and place them in plastic bags.
2. Give each student a bag of cotton balls.
3. Line them up 1-foot away from the can.
4. Demonstrate how to throw the cotton balls into the can.
5. Show how to make a game to take home by gluing the small hands to a foam cup.

Discuss
Say, Have you thanked Jesus for what He has done for you? We can thank Him when we pray. Let's fold our hands now and thank Jesus for His blessings.

God's Child Is Thankful

Prayer
Dear Jesus, thank You for giving me this special class. We want to thank You for the special things You have done for each one (name the things they mentioned). Together we say, "Thank You." (Have the class say "Thank You" together.) Amen.

65

Chapter 7
God's Child Is Content

Memory Verse

Be content with what you have. Hebrews 13:5

Story to Share
I Want More!

Naaman, the great leader of Syria's army, had a terrible disease. It was called leprosy. His wife was very sad.

"Why are you crying?" asked her maid.

"Oh, it is just terrible. Naaman has the dreaded disease. He has leprosy," she answered before covering her face with her hands and sobbing.

"Don't cry," said the little maid. "I know a great prophet, Elisha. He could cure your husband."

Naaman left on a journey to Elisha's home. Elisha sent his servant Gehazi to tell Naaman what to do: "Elisha says to go wash in the Jordan River seven times. Then your skin will be pure."

Naaman obeyed Elisha's orders and his skin became like that of a young boy. He was cured. Naaman was so thankful he tried to give Elisha some magnificent presents. "Thank you for helping to cure me of my leprosy," he said as he handed the gifts to Elisha. "I know your God must be the true God. Take these gifts and gold as my thank-you."

"No," said Elisha. "I don't want your gifts. May God bless you as you return to your home."

Gehazi heard Naaman offer Elisha the gifts. He wanted those beautiful presents! I'll just wait until Naaman is out of sight, he thought. Then I will go get the gifts.

That's what he did. As soon as Naaman was out of Elisha's sight, he hurried to him. "My master has changed his mind," he lied. "He would like the gifts and gold."

But God helped Elisha to know about Gehazi's sin. "You will have the curse of leprosy because you are not content with what you have," he told him.

Elisha knew how to be content with what God had given him. He was God's child.

— based on 2 Kings 5:15-27

Questions for Discussion

1. Was Gehazi satisfied with what he already had?
2. How do you feel about your toys, clothes and home? Are you satisfied with what you have?

Be Content

activity

• • • • • • • • • • • • •

Materials

- bee and toy patterns
- crayons
- glue
- craft sticks
- scissors

Directions

1. Before class, duplicate and cut out the bee and toy patterns, one set per child.
2. Instruct the students to color the bee and toys.
3. Show how to glue the bee and toys to the ends of craft sticks.
4. Say the memory verse, holding up the bee for "be" and the toys for "content."

Discuss

Ask, **How many of you have a toy box with toys in it? Maybe you keep your toys in your drawers or closet. Is there some toy you are wishing for? God tells us to be content with the toys we have. It's okay to get a new toy once in a while, but you shouldn't fuss for something new on each trip to a store. Remember, "Be content."**

God's Child Is Content

Buzzing Content Bees

finished craft

Materials
- stripes and eye patterns
- glue
- yellow round balloons
- scissors
- red permanent marker

Directions
1. Before class, duplicate and cut out the stripes and eye patterns, one set per student. Inflate a balloon for each child. Hint: Do not inflate the balloons to their fullest size — this will keep them from breaking easily. Have extras on hand just in case.
2. Show where to glue the eyes and stripes on the balloons (see illustration).
3. Help each child draw a mouth on the balloon (be especially careful with the permanent marker).
4. Throw the balloons up in the air, with everyone trying to hit them to keep them flying. In rhythm, say "Buzz, buzz, Be content. Buzz, Buzz, Be content."

God's Child Is Content

song

• • • • • • • • • • •

Materials
- signs
- poster board
- crayons
- scissors

Directions
1. Duplicate one Bee sign per child.
2. Give a Bee sign to each child and instruct the students to color the bees.
3. Have the children draw a toy on the back side of the sign.
4. Ask, **Do you know what it means to be content? It means to be satisfied with what you have. If you are content you won't wish for something new all the time. You will enjoy what you have already.**
5. Sing the "Bee Content" song to the tune of "Deep and Wide," holding up the Bee sign on the first verse and the toy side on the second verse.

God's Child Is Content

Bee Content

Be content with what you have.
Hebrews 13:5

Song

Be content.
Be content.
Be content with what you have.
Be content.
Be content.
Be content with what you have.

I'm content.
I'm content.
I'm content with what I have.
I'm content.
I'm content.
I'm content with what I have.

The Gift of Contentment

craft

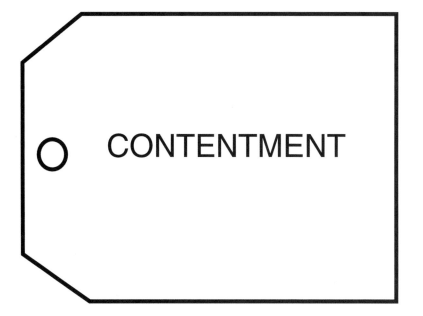

CONTENTMENT

CONTENTMENT

Materials

- gift tag
- small boxes with lids
- foil gift wrap
- self-stick gift bows
- self-stick magnets
- clear tape

Directions

1. Before class, duplicate and cut out a gift tag for each child.
2. Show how to wrap the box with gift wrap.
3. Give each student a tag and instruct him or her to tape it on the package.
4. Show where to stick on the bow.
5. Give each child a magnet to stick on the bottom or side of the box so it can hang on the refrigerator.

Discuss

Say, **The best gift you can give your friends is to teach them to be content. You can do that with this gift box you will make today. When you give the gift to your friend, tell your friend not to open the box but to put it where he or she will see it every day. It's to remind your friend to always be content.**

God's Child Is Content

Full Hearts

craft

Materials
- heart pattern
- brown paper grocery bags
- scissors
- red paint
- paint brushes
- paint smocks
- fiberfill stuffing
- small pictures of Jesus
- hole punch
- yarn

Directions

1. Trace the heart onto a bag and cut out two for each student. Cut the yarn into 8" lengths.
2. Have the children put on paint smocks. Allow them to paint one heart each.
3. Instruct them to glue a picture of Jesus to the middle of the painted heart. Say, **When we have Jesus in our hearts, He fills it so full that we don't have room for the "I wants."**
4. Show how to glue the edges of the heart, leaving a 3" open space.
5. Go around the room and stuff fiberfill in the hole. Help the students glue the hole closed. Punch a hole on the top of each heart. Tie a piece of yarn through the hole for hanging.

God's Child Is Content

Yummy Gifts of Contentment

activity/snack

• • • • • • • • • •

Materials

- placemat pattern
- scissors
- cheese chunks
- licorice strings
- crayons

Directions

1. Before class, duplicate and cut out a placemat for each child.
2. Instruct the children to draw the food on the empty plate that their parents fix for them to eat.
3. Assist the children in tying the licorice strings around their cheese chunks like gifts.

Discuss

Ask, **Are you content with what your parents fix for you to eat? Do you complain when you come to the table: "Green beans, yuck!" or " I hate meat loaf; why can't we have spaghetti?" God wants us to be satisfied with what we have and be thankful, too. Let's thank Him for our snack.** Offer prayer.

God's Child Is Content

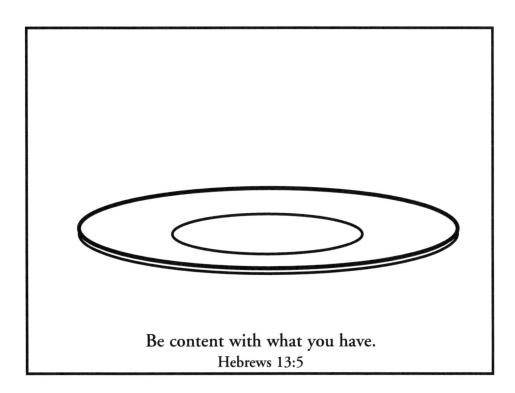

Be content with what you have.
Hebrews 13:5

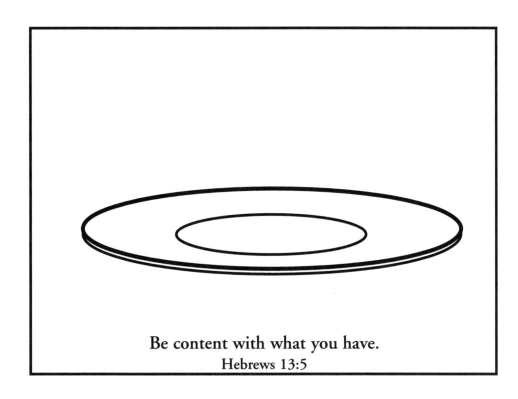

Be content with what you have.
Hebrews 13:5

activity

· · · · · · · · · · ·

Materials
- parent letter
- plain newsprint
- water-soluble ink pads, various colors
- paint smocks
- wet cloths

Directions
1. Before class, duplicate a letter for each child. Ask your pastor for information on needy children.
2. Help the children put on paint smocks to protect their clothing.
3. Give each child a large piece of newsprint and demonstrate how to decorate the paper using the ink pad and a finger to make hearts, animals, flowers, etc.
4. After the newsprint dries, sign and attach a parent letter and send them home with the children.

Discuss
Ask, **Do you have more toys and books than you need?** Wrap a toy in this special paper and give it to someone who doesn't have as much as you. God likes when we give to others.

God's Child Is Content

Gifts for Others

Dear Parent,
Our class is learning to be content! Your child has discussed the toys in his/her toy box and has discovered he/she could get along without some of them. This special gift wrap is for an item your child will select for a needy child. If you do not know of a needy child for the gift I will be happy to assist you in finding someone through our church.

Thank you,

_____ and your contented child,

_____

Dear Parent,
Our class is learning to be content! Your child has discussed the toys in his/her toy box and has discovered he/she could get along without some of them. This special gift wrap is for an item your child will select for a needy child. If you do not know of a needy child for the gift I will be happy to assist you in finding someone through our church.

Thank you,

_____ and your contented child,

_____

Dear Parent,
Our class is learning to be content! Your child has discussed the toys in his/her toy box and has discovered he/she could get along without some of them. This special gift wrap is for an item your child will select for a needy child. If you do not know of a needy child for the gift I will be happy to assist you in finding someone through our church.

Thank you,

_____ and your contented child,

_____

Naaman's Spots

Materials
- Naaman and leprosy spots
- sticky tack
- crayons
- blindfold

Directions
1. Cut out and color Naaman and attach him to a wall. Duplicate and cut out one leprosy spot per child. This game is similar to Pin the Tail on the Donkey.
2. Blindfold a child, give him or her a leprosy spot.
3. Turn the child in two complete circles and instruct him or her to put the spot on Naaman.
4. Write each child's name on a spot and see how many of the spots land on Naaman.

Usage
Lay the Naaman figure and some crayons on the table for early birds to color.

God's Child Is Content

Chapter 8
God's Child Is Happy

Memory Verse

Be joyful always. 1 Thessalonians 5:16

Story to Share
Happy, Happy Shepherd

David was a shepherd boy. He took his father's sheep to the hills around Bethlehem and watched over them. When it stormed, David was out with his sheep. One night during a loud storm David sang, "Bless the Lord, Thou art very great, You walk on the wings of the wind."

Being a shepherd was a lonely life. And sometimes it was scary, too. One day David heard, "Baaa, Baaa." It sounded like a lamb was saying, "Help me, help me." When David turned around he saw a bear carrying a lamb in his teeth.

"Stop," shouted David. He quickly put a smooth stone in his sling and whirled it around his head. As he let go of one end of the sling, the stone flew through the air and hit the bear.

David ran toward the stunned bear and grabbed the lamb out of the bear's mouth. Furious, the bear ran toward David. "Help me, Father God," prayed David. He grabbed the bear, hit it and watched as the bear fell to the ground. It was dead! "Thank You, God, thank You," David said.

Even when David was afraid or lonely, he knew God was with him. He wrote many songs to sing to God. One day when all of the lambs were lying quietly on the green grass, David played his harp and sang, "The Lord is my shepherd, I shall not be in want."

David was a happy shepherd boy. He was God's child.

— based on Psalm 23

Questions for Discussion
1. Do you like to sing while you are playing? Do you sing because you are happy?
2. Do you think your family is happy when you are happy?

Mirror, Mirror

Materials

- mirror and insert patterns
- scissors
- poster board
- aluminum foil
- glue
- hand-held mirror

Directions

1. Duplicate and cut out a mirror for each child from poster board and a mirror insert from aluminum foil.
2. Show how to glue the foil to the poster board mirror.

Discuss

Ask, **Did you ever look in the mirror and see an unhappy child? Pass the real mirror around. Say, Look in this mirror. What do you see? Frowns or happy faces? How do you feel when you see your friend wear a frown? Do you feel different when you see a smile? God's Word, the Bible says, "Be joyful always,"** so when you look in the mirror, remember to say, **"Mirror, mirror on the wall, do I have the biggest smile of all?"**

God's Child Is Happy

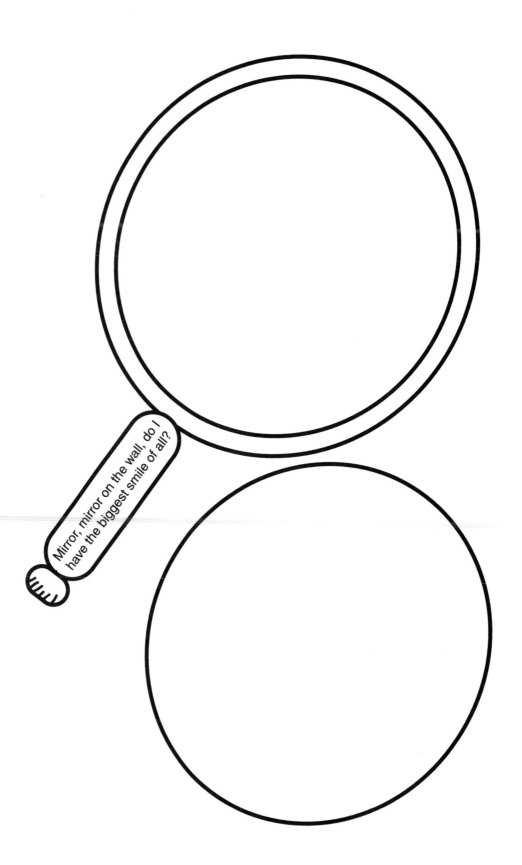

Mirror, mirror on the wall, do I have the biggest smile of all?

Color by Number

puzzle

· · · · · · · · · · ·

Materials
• activity sheet
• crayons

Directions
1. Before class, duplicate one activity sheet per child.
2. Say, **Number 1 is brown, number 2 is blue, number 3 is green and number 4 is yellow.**

Usage
Color the crayon tips on the activity sheets the correct color so the students will be able to easily match the numbers to the colors.

craft

· · · · · · · · · · · ·

Materials

- lamb
- heavy paper or poster board
- scissors
- hole punch
- yarn
- clear tape
- crayons
- clear, self-stick paper (optional)

Directions

1. Before class, duplicate and cut out a lamb for each child. Punch holes where indicated on the lambs. Cut the yarn into 24" lengths. Wrap tape around the ends. Tie one end of the yarn to a hole in the lamb.
2. Allow the students to color the lamb.
3. Demonstrate how to "sew" around the lamb.

Usage

For a longer-lasting sewing card, cover it with clear, self-stick paper.

God's Child Is Happy

Lamb Sewing Card

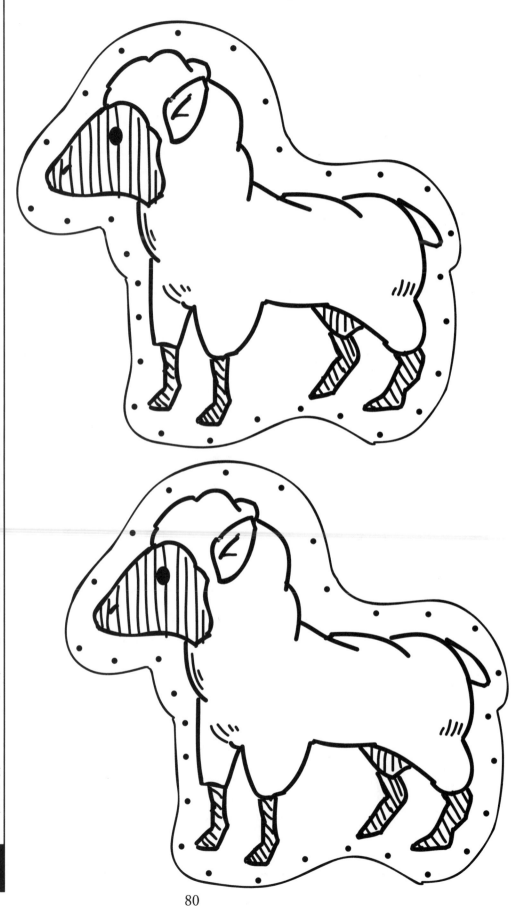

Take-Home Reminder

Materials
- lamb and parent note
- scissors
- resealable plastic sandwich bags
- cotton balls
- self-stick magnets

Directions
1. Before class, duplicate and cut out a lamb and parent note for each child. Sign the notes. Slightly pull apart the cotton and place seven cotton balls in a bag for each child.
2. Provide each child with a lamb, a bag of cotton balls and a parent note.
3. Distribute the magnets and instruct the students to glue one to the back of the lamb.
4. Say, **You can take your lamb home with these cotton balls. His name is Snowflake. Every day that you remember to be happy, glue a cotton ball to S n o w f l a k e. Snowflake will be happy, too, when he has his wool to keep him warm.**

God's Child Is Happy

Dear Parent,
Snowflake wants to help me be happy all week. Will you help me glue a cotton ball to my lamb each day I am happy? The Bible says to "Be joyful always." I want to be God's happy child.

XOXO,

_____

All Sizes

Materials

- activity sheet
- scissors
- glue
- crayons

Directions

1. Before class, duplicate the adult and child figures and cut them out, one set per child. Then duplicate the lamb picture for each child.
2. Instruct the class to color the picture and the figures.
3. Have the children glue the father figure by the father lamb on the activity sheet. They should do the same with the mother and baby figures.

Discuss

Ask, **Who can be joyful always? Do you have to be a certain size?** (as tall as Pastor, tall enough to reach the light switch, etc.) **Do you have to be a certain age?** (10, 20, 30?) **No, it doesn't matter how big or how old you are: you can be joyful always!**

God's Child Is Happy

Be joyful always.
1 Thessalonians 5:16

Happy Lambs

Be joyful always.
1 Thessalonians 5:16

activity

. . . .

Materials

• activity sheet
• crayons

Directions

1. Before class, dupli-cate the activity sheet for each child.
2. Help the students count the lambs, then have them trace the 10.
3. Instruct the students to color two lambs red, two lambs blue, two lambs pink, two lambs green and two lambs yellow.

Discuss

Ask, **Do the lambs on this page look happy? Why do you think they are kicking up their heels? Can you see the juicy grass? Can you see the cool water? Can you see the kind shepherd? What do you have to be happy about?**

God's Child Is Happy

Baaa-by

activity

· · · · · · · · · · · ·

Materials

- lamb mask
- large $1/4$" rubber bands
- stapler
- clear tape
- scissors

Directions

1. Before class, duplicate and cut out a lamb mask for each child.
2. Cut each rubber band to make one long piece. Staple the ends to the mask sides. Cover the staples with tape to avoid injury.
3. Lead the students in "bleating" the verse: "Beeeeee jooooooyful aaaal-waaaays."

David's Bears

puzzle

· · · · · · · · · · ·

Materials
- activity sheet
- crayons

Directions
1. Before class, duplicate the activity sheet for each child.
2. Instruct the children to match a standing bear to a dead bear by drawing a line from one to the other.
3. Say, **Look at all of these different bears. One reason I'm so happy is because all of you here are different. You are just yourself — not like anyone else — and that makes me happy.**

God's Child Is Happy

Chapter 9
Miscellaneous Activities

Guess what happened to me today?

My teacher, _____,

could tell I, _____,

 was God's child because I

_____

_____

_____

Date:_____

Guess what happened to me today?

My teacher, _____,

could tell I, _____,

 was God's child because I

_____

_____

_____

Date:_____

Guess what happened to me today?

My teacher, _____,

could tell I, _____,

 was God's child because I

_____

_____

_____

Date:_____

Guess what happened to me today?

My teacher, _____,

could tell I, _____,

 was God's child because I

_____

_____

_____

Date:_____

It Doesn't Belong

puzzle

Materials
- activity sheet
- crayons

Directions
1. Before class, duplicate the activity sheet for each student.
2. Instruct the students to make an X on the item in each row that does not belong. Suggest that they color the two that match.

God's Children Wiggle Buster

action rhyme

. . . .

Directions

1. Say the rhyme as you do the actions.
2. Have the class repeat it with you until they learn the rhyme and actions.

God's children sometimes wiggle,
> *wiggle all over*

Or even get the giggles,
> *cover mouth and giggle*

But they all have a great big heart.
> *make a big heart in the air*

So get ready to start.
> *jumping jack yelling "I'm God's Child"*

God's Child Heart

craft

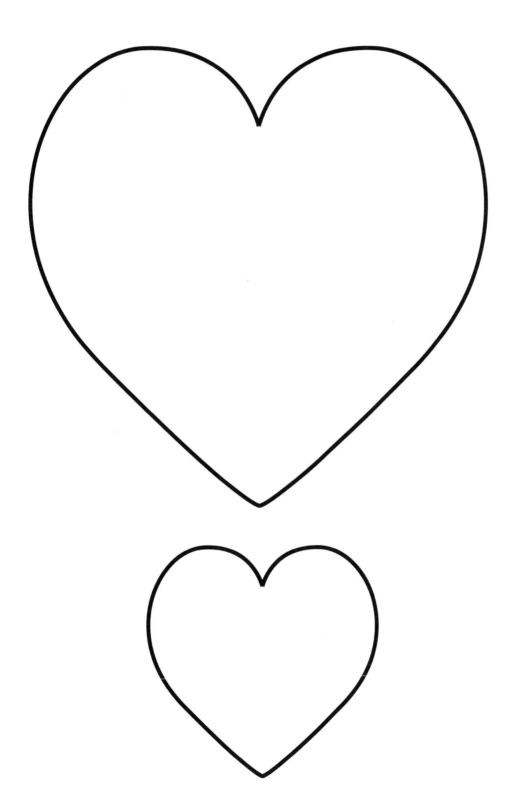

Materials
- small and large hearts
- white and red paper
- glue
- scissors
- yarn
- hole punch

Directions
1. Before class, duplicate and cut out a small heart from white paper and a large heart from red paper. Punch a hole at the top of the large heart. Cut the yarn into 24" lengths.
2. Instruct the students to glue the small heart to the middle of the big heart.
3. Help the children thread the yarn through the hole. Assist them in tying it at the top.

game

• • • • • • • • • • •

Materials

- memory cards
- poster board
- clear, self-stick plastic
- scissors
- colored pencils or markers

Directions

1. Duplicate the memory cards to make two of each and color them.
2. Cover them with the clear, self-stick plastic and cut them out.
3. Lay the cards face down in the middle of the table.
4. Have a student pick up two cards. If the cards do not match, the student should return them to the table. If they do match, and the student can tell something about that lesson, he should keep the cards.
5. The one with the most cards at the end of the game wins.

Usage

Consider making additional copies so the students can take a game home with them. Provide resealable plastic bags to keep the pieces together.

Memory Review

We're Friends of God

bulletin board

· · · · · · · · · ·

Materials

- frame and border
- poster board
- scissors
- glue
- picture of Jesus
- colored paper
- markers or crayons
- stapler

Directions

1. Cover the bulletin board with yellow paper.
2. Duplicate the flower border and cut it out. Color the flowers. Attach them around the bulletin board.
3. Attach a picture of Jesus to the center of the bulletin board.
4. Duplicate and cut out a frame for each student. Allow them to color the frame.
5. Cut snapshots of each child to 3" x 4" and glue them to backs of the frames.
6. Freehand cut or trace lettering to say "We're Friends of God" and attach it to the top of the bulletin board.
7. As you add each child's photo, say, **Here is a friend of God.**

Dear Parent,

We are making a special bulletin board of God's Children. Please send a snapshot of your child to class that can be cut to 3" x 4". Your child will bring the picture home at the end of our series. We would be happy to have you stop by to see our bulletin board during these lessons.

Thank you,

_____

teacher

Dear Parent,

We are making a special bulletin board of God's Children. Please send a snapshot of your child to class that can be cut to 3" x 4". Your child will bring the picture home at the end of our series. We would be happy to have you stop by to see our bulletin board during these lessons.

Thank you,

_____

teacher

God's Child

● ● ● ● ● ● ● ● ● ●

Materials
- girl and boy signs
- glue
- crayons
- craft sticks
- scissors

Directions

1. Duplicate and cut out the boy and girl signs.
2. Distribute a boy or girl sign to the students.
3. Instruct them to color their signs.
4. Demonstrate how to glue a craft stick to the back of the sign to make it sturdy.
5. Assist the children in writing their names on the sign.
6. Sing "God's Child" to the tune of "Are You Sleeping" as each child holds up the sign when you sing his or her name.

Song

_____ is God's child.

_____ is God's child.

Yes he is.

Yes he is.

He lives for God each day,

Takes time to read and pray.

He's God's child.

He's God's child.

Miscellaneous Activities

96